Collected Thoughts: Curated Writings, Musings, Ideas, & Ramblings

Brigitte Beam

BookLeaf Publishing

India | USA | UK

Presentation by *BookLeaf Publishing*

Web: www.bookleafpub.com

E-mail: info@bookleafpub.com

ISBN: 9789360947439

First edition 2024

*I want to give a simple thank you.
Sometimes, thank you's are never simple.
But here it goes: thank you for always being
my Lorelia to my Rory even when I'm more
like Lorelia and you're like Rory. To my
Gilmore Girl. Thank you.*

Spill the Tea

Spill the tea
Tell me
Tell me

Will it be
Anything
Like the Boston party

Tell me
Tell me

Is it anything
Like the
Mad Hatter's
At half past three

Spill the tea
Tell me
Tell me
Tell me you remember
Tea stains

Sticks and Stones

Why do the say
Sticks and stones
May break
Break your bones
But words
Will never hurt me

Words hurt
Truth hurts
Lies hurt
Life hurts

I'd rather have
Broken
Broken bones

Than a broken mind
Broken spirit
Broken chance
A broken life

Why can't everyone just be nice

We can't be friends

We can't be friends
It's really not you,
It's you and you and me
I just know I won't be free

Peer pressure is true
I always thought
My mom was talking
About drugs
And not about you

We can't be friends
We both know
How this will end

Technicolor

Why can't everything be
In black and white
Just like all the best movies

Everything is smudged
With grey
Faded yellow
Like memories

But, I
Can remember
Plain as day
The technicolor
Just like any other

Reality

There's no white horse
There's no enemy
There's just this one person focused on me

Is this real
Or just a dream

This is a fairytale
Made of white
Created by my imagination
Come to life

It's a picture in black
And white
It's reality
Back on track

There are dragons
Bigger than me

And a prince charming
That almost
Was like
Could not
Never

Be

This fantasy is cursed
And will never immerse
To reality

It's not okay

But it's not okay to push me
It's not okay to pick
It's not okay to pick and rip
It's not okay to pick at that scab

You're gonna make me bleed
Bleed more than I need
You just want to see
See the red in my veins

Devils advocate in my head

When I've already gone over all our
conversations before I've even talked to you
And it turns out none of those possibilities could
be true

These arguments aren't worth the candle
The wax is burning my hand
And I just don't understand

But that doesn't mean that I don't want you right
to the left of me
It's not right

And it's not okay
Okay

Autumn

Black and red ink on your skin
Gold leaf sprinkled in your hair
And cloaked in a worn black leather jacket

White autumn leaves
Fall on the ground

Saving Superman

We need to stop saving Superman
He already thinks
He does good better than we can
Keep him occupied
Keep him far off land

We can always say we tried
There should be nothing
To hide

Stop saving Superman
Maybe he can do better
Than we can

Her

Chase her
Even when she's already yours
Give her a thousand yellow daisies
Even if she drives you crazy
Love her
Everyday more than your last
But most importantly,
Choose her
Like she chose you

Anxiety

The tightness in my chest
Gets heavier and heavier
Like you are putting dirt
Dirt on my grave
Burying me alive

Feels like I'm Tom Sawyer
Watching
Waiting
At my own funeral
But I
I can't do anything
I can't move

The waves are washing me under
Keeping me under
Under tow

But I can't breathe
Gasping for air
That you can't see
Isn't it a shame about the crippling anxiety

Neighbor

Don't they say
Love thy
Love thy neighbor

Even if I
I don't like
Like my neighbor

There's not a
A tall enough fence
To keep
Keep Petunia Dursley
Out

1.2.3

One
Two
Three
You and me

Four
Five
Six
Hug and kiss

Pillow Talk Poet

You're a
Pillow talk poet
Whispering
Sweet nothings in my ear

You're a
Dry cleaner's nightmare
With that brand of lipstick on your collar

You're a
Cheaters that's been caught
With not my shade
Of red
Handed

I have to give
A hand to you
You're a
Pillow talk poet

President

You told me
I could be
President

Why would
I be
When they
Represent
Everything
That is free

When I
Don't feel
Free
To be me
To be seen
To be heard

Wishing Star

17

How many wishes
Does the single
Star have

Is it's twinkle
A wave
From billions of
Light years away

Flower Bomb

I'm not delicate
Like a flower
But I detonate
Like a bomb

Roses are red
Violets can be violent
Even when you think
They are silent

I'm not fragile
Like a flower
I can scream
Like a child

Do you hear me
Or do you, only
See the
Aftermath
Unfortunately

Raindrops fell

Raindrops fell
From my eyes
As a teardrop
Broke
From the sky
Alice is never
Never the right size

Alarm clock

Alarm clock ringing
Racing to get ready
I'm gonna be late
Again
I always think
Snooze is my best friend

I can't wait

I can't wait
Wait to
Forget you
Like the chipped nail polish
I don't know where or when it went
So insignificant
I forgot about the time spent
There's not point in being melancholic
Or blue
So very true
Can you relate

Van Gogh

Even though
Van Gogh
Didn't paint
The sky blue

I know he'd paint
Sunflowers
In your eyes
Possibly a stippling smile

And after awhile,
You'd know
That I love you

Hey Stranger

Hey stranger
Is what
You use to call me
When I was no older
Than seventeen

Hey stranger
Is what
You use to say
When we'd both
Been at school all day

Hey stranger
Is what
You say
When we'd take
Our walks
Every Wednesday

Back when
We'd chat
About trivial things
When you
Controlled
Your stutter

And I'd try
To perfect everything

Back when
Things stayed simple
When you were shorter
And I thought
Things worth getting
Would always
Come easily

Back when
You wouldn't stop
Stop talking
Why don't you talk
Talk to me now
You use to look up at me
And now
I can only think
You look down

Most of the time
I don't like you
But I love you

I love
Love the stranger
I don't know

Hey stranger
Why are we
We still strangers

www.ingramcontent.com/pod-product-compliance
Lightning Source LLC
LaVergne TN
LVHW021357200726
843509LV00014B/2902